Communication Activity Guide

Arlie the Alligator

by Sandra Warren

Script and Music

Readers' Theater

Exploring Communication through Classroom Activities and Projects

Pieces of Learning

Division of Creative Learning Consultants

© 1993 Creative Learning
Consultants Inc.
ISBN 0-9623835-9-7

Edited by
Kathy Balsamo
Graphic Production
Pat Bleidorn
Cover alligator by
Deborah Thomas

Communication Activity Guide
Arlie the Alligator

"Arlie the Alligator"
"I Love the Sandy Beach"
"Daddy Always Taught Me
    to Bellow"
"If It's the Last Thing I Do"

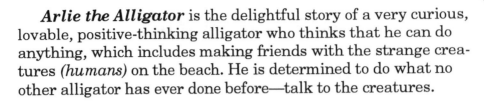

Introduction

Arlie the Alligator is the delightful story of a very curious, lovable, positive-thinking alligator who thinks that he can do anything, which includes making friends with the strange creatures *(humans)* on the beach. He is determined to do what no other alligator has ever done before—talk to the creatures.

Communication is vital to **our** existence as human beings. *Arlie's* story motivates children to think about the importance of communication in **their** daily lives. *Arlie's* struggle to speak to the strange creatures is no different than the struggle and frustration one person feels trying to communicate concerns to another—parent to child; student to student; student to teacher.

Before or after encountering *Arlie,* this **Communication Activity Guide** allows students to experience cross-curriculum activities as an integral part of *Arlie's* story.

Primary students will enjoy listening to the *audio tape* of *Arlie the Alligator* and can read-along with the four-color *hardback library edition.* They will enjoy singing along with *Arlie* and participating in the musical productions.

Intermediate students will enjoy being a part of the **Readers' Theater** or play and may wish to present the production to primary students. They may also enjoy sharing the knowledge they gain and resulting products from the many communication activities. In productions, students will be able to help *Arlie* develop a way to communicate with the strange creatures.

The objectives of a production include learning how:

* to stage
* to produce
* to act
* to sing in a musical
* to stimulate creative and productive thinking
* to develop a sensitivity to the many ways humans communicate with each other and the world around us.

This **Communication Activity Guide—Arlie the Alligator** is one of a three-part package. Other components of the package include a four-color library edition story book *Arlie the Alligator* and an audio tape of the complete production. *Arlie the Alligator* is a story to read—a tape to listen to—a mini-musical to perform—and a lesson in communication. The audio tape and hardback edition are available from *Arlie Enterprises*— see page 79.

The Musical

Production Suggestions

Stage this mini-musical as simply or as elaborately as you and your primary and intermediate students wish. Change or add to this production to involve more students. Expand roles by having one child perform a character's speaking role and another the singing role while still others pantomime what is being said and sung. In each song you can change the pronouns and have the entire choir or small groups sing. There are six speaking roles. Two of those roles also sing:

Characters	Characteristics
ARLIE:	(*speaking and singing*) bright, cheery, positive; yellow markings on the costume are important to the script
NARRATOR:	(*speaking*) smooth reader, good speaking voice; able to express emotion
FATHER:	(*speaking and singing*) lower speaking voice preferred
MOTHER:	(*speaking*) sweet voice, comforting
CHILD:	(*speaking*) as curious as Arlie
FRIEND:	(*speaking*)

You can divide the **NARRATOR** script into several smaller parts to involve more students. Several children can share the **FRIEND** speaking part that in unison warns **Arlie.**

There are four songs included in this production.

Arlie the Alligator - Theme song (Choir)

I Love the Sandy Beach - (Arlie)

Daddy Always Taught Me to Bellow - (Arlie and Father)

If It's the Last Thing I Do - (Arlie)

- Basic decisions about staging depend upon the available facilities, staff and parental support, financial support and the limits of your imagination. Involve the students in designing and making backdrops, props, costumes, tickets, advertising posters and brochures. Encourage their creativity in planning this musical production or Readers' Theater. It need not be costly. It should be FUN!

- The beach can be the stage or gymnasium floor, bare or covered with a beige sheet or real sand. The reeds or tall grass that **Arlie** peeks through might be real plants borrowed from the office, artificial greenery, or long grass created, painted, and cut from paper or cardboard.

- Make simple costumes:

Posters:	Make and carry; or pin on a poster for each character
Paper masks:	Color or paint a mask depicting each character. Attach to coat hangers for strength. (Remember speaking behind a mask is difficult.)

Hats:	**Arlie** wears a green hat; **Father** wears a construction hard hat. Let students suggest other characters' hats.
Tee-shirts:	Use different colors for each character. Children can tie-dye shirts as a class project. Or they can draw the trunk of their character on the shirt.
Strange Creatures:	Wear beach wear (bathing suits, shorts, tee-shirts, and carry towels, pails, shovels, sun glasses, coolers, frisbees, beach umbrellas, beach balls, etc.)

- The strange creatures on the beach can be the entire choir or a small group of students. For a real twist or treat for the children, the strange creatures could be some of the **TEACHERS** dressed in outlandish beach outfits, mismatched of course! For beach sounds use professional audio tapes or have a group of students create and perform and tape record the sound effects (ocean sounds, birds chirping and the tide flowing in and out).

- Expand the script or Readers' Theater to include more students, to lengthen, to help meet specific needs or goals. Good places to add dialogue and/or action are:

  — Add an introduction before **Arlie the Alligator** (perhaps some children laughing and talking about what fun they are going to have on the beach).

  — Expand on the dialog of **Arlie's FRIENDS** and what they are trying to tell him.

  — Throughout *I Love the Sandy Beach* have different students share the narration lines.

  — After *I Love the Sandy Beach* add to **Arlie's** description of the creatures. What other things might people be doing on the beach?

  — After *I Love the Sandy Beach*, verse 2, add to the **NARRATOR'S** description of the activities on the beach.

  — Add **NARRATOR** at the end of the song and have the student speak about how humans communicate with animals. Have **NARRATOR** challenge those in the audience to develop in their minds a means of communication for **Arlie**.

  — Add a final scene with **Arlie** figuring out how to communicate with the creatures.

  — Instead of singing all the songs, have students recite them using their own "rap" rhythm. Divide students into small groups. Each group can create a new "rap."

  — Add a song written by students: Challenge students to write a 3-verse, 4-line rhyming poem. Have them recite it, listening for the rhythm of the words. Create a melody to accompany the poem.

  — Rewrite the words to popular songs from an alligator's point of view.

  — For the curtain call, sing the theme song twice. The first time do as a Readers' Theater involving the audience. The second time invite the audience to sing with the cast.

  — Sing the entire theme song for the curtain call.

  — Sign one or all of the songs.

The Musical Script

The stage is split with tall grass and sand on one side and the strange creatures (humans) on the other. The strange creatures are going through the motions of playing, digging, and swimming, but all is silent. *Arlie* slithers onto the stage looking very curious about everything around him. *Arlie* wiggles from side to side trying to get a better look at the strange creatures. Movements are confident yet cautious. Throughout the script *Arlie* is referred to as *he*. *Arlie* can be either female or male. Change pronouns where necessary.

Theme Song—Arlie the Alligator

Who is the alligator of a different kind?
Arlie, Oh Arlie the alligator.
Who is the one who is so curious to find out
everything his mind can hold?

Arlie, Oh Arlie, is filled with such curiosity.
Oh Arlie, Oh Arlie, where will your adventures lead?

Who is the alligator always with a smile?
Arlie, Oh Arlie the alligator.
Who is the one who's there to crawl the extra mile,
To share a thought with you and me?

Oh Arlie, Oh Arlie, is filled with such curiosity.
Oh Arlie, Oh Arlie, where will your adventures lead?
Where will your adventures lead?
Where will your adventures lead? Arlie! Arlie!

(As narration begins, two or three of *Arlie's* friends enter and move towards *Arlie* from behind.)

NARRATOR: Arlie slithered onto the beach to enjoy the warm sun.

FRIENDS: Oh no, Arlie, don't go! You'll get into trouble!

(*Arlie* sticks *his* nose up in the air and moves forward not even looking at *his* friends.)

NARRATOR: Arlie paid no attention. *He* loved new experiences and was very curious about the unusual creatures found at the beach. Besides, *he* could take care of *himself*.

(Slowly, quietly, the strange creatures begin to make sounds—laughter, play sounds.)

He could hear the laughter of the city folk as they played in the sand nearby. Excitement welled up inside *him* as *he* carefully peered through the tall grass.

Musical Script Reproducible

I Love the Sandy Beach

(Sung by *Arlie*)

I love the sandy beach, cool water and warm sun.
Hiding behind this reed can be a lot of fun.
Watching creatures big and small, laugh and play and run.
How I wish I could be friends with every single one.

NARRATOR: Arlie watched for awhile, fascinated by all the different things that *he* saw.

(As **Arlie** describes the creatures, have them parade on stage starting with someone tall (on stilts maybe?), someone short, someone thin and someone rather portly.)

ARLIE: What strange creatures they are! All different sizes and shapes. Some are tall, some short, some thin as a reed and some rather portly! Alligators aren't like this at all. They are either short like me, or growing longer like my big brother and sister, or even longer like my Mom and Dad.

(As the Narrator talks, **Arlie** looks from *his* body to the creatures as if trying to compare *his* with theirs.)

NARRATOR: Arlie knew that *he* would lose *his* beautiful yellow markings when *he* grew up. All alligators do. But otherwise, *he* would look just like all the others. You almost had to be another alligator to tell them apart.

(As the Narrator continues, have creatures pretend to dig with pails and shovels, playing catch, swimming, etc.)

He loved to watch the creatures because they did such strange things. The shorter ones were putting sand in round containers and moving them all about.

(Students with pails and shovels pretend they are playing in the sand.)

Some were building with them.
Others were throwing things,

(Students with pails and shovels put their backs to the audience while pretending to play in the sand. They move aside and reveal a huge sand castle—made out of cardboard.)

(Two students play catch with a beach ball. Also a couple throw a frisbee—Make waves out of cardboard. Have students jump over the waves, walk in the water, and pretend to swim.)

walking in the water and even trying to
swim . . . like an alligator.

Song No. 2 con't.— I Love the Sandy Beach

(Sung by *Arlie*)

Some are twirling flat round saucers high up in the air.
Lots of little ones are digging in the sand out there.

NARRATOR: *He* even saw some playing alligator! They were lying in the sand, just like Arlie liked to do.

(Students on lawn chairs, sunbathing.)

ARLIE: How very interesting!

I love the sandy beach, cool water and warm sun.
I like to watch the creatures laugh and play and run.

(A child walks up to *Arlie* and puts *his* toes in front of *Arlie's* snout. The size of the feet are exaggerated because of the angle. Lower the lights. Use a spot light behind the child so like *Arlie*, the audience is blinded by the light. Use exaggerated big feet to show the illusion of the enormous black objects. Use a kettle drum roll or cymbal noises to enhance the suspense.)

NARRATOR: SUDDENLY . . . a dark shadow fell across Arlie's path, blocking *his* view. Right before *his* eyes were the strangest looking objects *he* had ever seen! Ten round wiggly bumps attached to two towering stalks were staring right into *his* snout!

(*Arlie* reacts in a startled, surprised manner.)

ARLIE: Oh my! Oh my! What could this be?

NARRATOR: *He* was too curious to be frightened.

CHILD: Hello Mr. Alligator, what'cha doing?

(Arlie reacts by leaning way back looking, up at the child.)

NARRATOR: Arlie leaned back as far as *he* could, trying to see where the voice was coming from. *His* heart was pounding loudly.

Musical Script Reproducible

Division of Creative Learning Consultants © 1993

(Use a drum for *Arlie's* beating heart or have the choir say in unison, "Thump, Thump, Thump, Thump." *Arlie* reacts with excitement!)

ARLIE: Oh my goodness! It's one of the little creatures!

(The child leans over and greets *Arlie* again.)

CHILD: I said, hello Mr. Alligator, what are you doing here?

(**Arlie** looks around as if trying to decide what to do.)

ARLIE: Oh dear me! I wish I could understand what it is saying. I am sure it is trying to be friends. What should I do? What shall I do?

Daddy Always Taught Me to Bellow

(Sung)Arlie:

What shall I do?
I've never been in a situation like this.
What shall I do?
I wish I could get a clue.
Let me think a moment or two.

What would my sister do?
What would my brother do?
What would my best friend do?
There must be some way to get my message across
before it's too late!
What would my mother do?
What would my father do?
What would my father do?

Wait!   By gosh!   By golly!   I got it!   It's true!
Daddy always taught me to bellow, to bellow, to bellow!
Daddy always taught me to bellow! "Hey fellow," he'd say!

Father:

One day when you grow up my son,
You will be as large as me.
And, you might find that you'll have the urge . . .
To say a word or two or three.

Arlie:

> *Daddy always taught me to bellow, to bellow, to bellow!*
> *Daddy always taught me to bellow! "Hey fellow," he'd say.*

Father:

> *You're great, great, great Grand-gator,*
> *Was quite the communicator.*
> *He discovered a way to express, what*
> *He felt he had to say . . .*

Choir:

> *Daddy always taught me to bellow, to bellow, to bellow!*
> *Daddy always taught me to bellow!*
> *"Hey fellow . . . BBBEEELLLLOOOOOOOOWWWWWWW!*

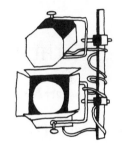

(*Arlie* moves with the narration.)

NARRATOR: So, Arlie leaned way back,

(The choir leans back with *Arlie*.)

took a GREAT BIG GIGUNDOUS BREATH,

(The choir takes an audible breath, inhaling.)

and let out the loudest BELLLLLOOOOOOOOOOOOOOOOWWWWWW anyone had ever heard.

(The choir and *Arlie* bellow together. As this happens, everyone on stage freezes their movements. They then slowly turn their heads to look at *Arlie*.)

It was so loud that all the alligators stopped what they were doing. Even the creatures on the beach turned to look.

Arlie's parents moved quickly to *his* side.

(*Arlie's* parents move close in a protective manner.)

PARENTS: Arlie, are you all right?

(One of the strange creatures grabs the young child and whisks the child away. The creatures begin to scream — "HELP! Alligator! Run for your life!" quietly at first, building slowly but never loud enough to drown out the Narrator.)

NARRATOR: At the same time, a larger creature swooped up Arlie's new friend and ran in the opposite direction. Arlie bellowed once more.

ARLIE: Wait! Please wait! Oh, I didn't mean to frighten you!

(*Arlie* looks in disbelief, embarrassed yet sad and apologetic.)

NARRATOR: But it was too late. All the creatures were screaming and yelling and running down the beach.

(Screaming sounds slowly fade as the choir exits the stage. *Arlie's* parents are at *his* side.)

ARLIE: Gosh, I didn't mean to scare anyone.

MOTHER: We know that. Other alligators have tried to communicate with the creatures, but no one has ever gotten through to them.

FATHER: You were very brave to try. We are proud of you.

(*Arlie's* parents move towards the stage exit.)

MOTHER: Time for some fresh seaweed pie. You've had enough excitement for one day.

(Arlie slowly turns to leave. *He* looks back just before leaving the stage.)

NARRATOR: As *he* paddled off towards home, Arlie looked back one more time.

ARLIE: The creature was trying to be friends. I am sure of it.

NARRATOR: Right then and there, Arlie made a promise to himself . . .

If It's the Last Thing I Do

(Sung by *Arlie*)

If it's the last thing I do, I will get through.
I would like to communicate.
Where there's a will there's a way,
And I know it's true, I must find out how to relate.

I understand . . . I need a plan.
And it may take some time, but I really don't mind.
Cuz there must be much we can share, if we only knew how.
If we could only break through the barrier,

I'm sure there's lots in common we could talk about.
And I'll make this a challenge to conquer.
And I'll make this a challenge to meet.
And as long as I believe in myself and don't give up,
I'll never see defeat.

If it's the last thing I do I will get through.
I would like to communicate. Where there's a will there's a way,
And I know it's true, I must find out how to relate!

ARLIE: If it's the last thing I do, I will get through to my friend!

(*Arlie* turns and paddles off stage.)

(OPTIONAL: NARRATOR addition below or create your own.)

NARRATOR: We, as human beings talk to animals all of the time. Our dogs and cats and horses and parrots—all of our pets—seem to understand us. But what if they really could talk to us? Would they like the way we treat them? What do you think they would tell us? As you return to your classroom, think about **Arlie** and *his* friend. What suggestions do you have to help **Arlie** get through to the strange creatures?

This musical was brought to you courtesy of . . . We would like to thank the following persons for their support and assistance . . We hope you have enjoyed meeting **Arlie** the Alligator.

FINALE BEGINS:

(Have cast return during the singing of the final song, *Arlie the Alligator,* for the curtain call. Start with the strange creatures, then Mother and Father, the Child, Friends and finally *Arlie.* Sing the entire song.)

Finale—Arlie the Alligator

(Sung by ALL)

Oh Arlie, Oh Arlie,
Is filled with such curiosity.
Oh Arlie, Oh Arlie,
Where will your adventures lead?
Where will your adventures lead?
Where will your adventures lead? Arlie, Arlie.

Arlie the Alligator

Words and Music by
DEBORAH BEL PFLEGER

♩ = 104

Who is the al-li-ga-tor of a dif-f'rent kind.
Who is the al-li-ga-tor al-ways with a smile.

Ar-lie, oh, Ar-lie, the al-li-ga-tor who is the one who is so cur-i-ous to find out
Ar-lie, oh, Ar-lie, the al-li-ga-tor who is the one who's there to crawl the ex-tra mile to

ev-'ry-thing his mind will hold. Oh, Ar-lie, oh, Ar-lie, is
share a thought with you and me. Oh, Ar-lie, oh, Ar-lie, is

14

I Love the Sandy Beach

Words and Music by
DEBORAH BEL PFLEGER

I love the sand - y beach, cool wa - ter and warm sun.

Hid - ing be - hind this reed can be a lot of fun.

Watch - ing crea - tures big and small laugh and play and run.

How I wish I could be friends with ev - 'ry sin - gle one.

NARRATOR: Arlie watched for awhile, fascinated by all the different things that he saw.

ARLIE: What strange creatures they are! All different sizes and shapes. Some are tall, some short, some thin as a reed and some rather portly! Alligators aren't like this at all. They are either short like me, or growing longer like my big brother and sister, or even looonnnger like my Mom and Dad.

NARRATOR: Arlie knew that he would lose his beautiful yellow markings when he grew up, all the alligators do. But otherwise, he would look just like all the others. You almost had to be another alligator to tell them apart.

He loved to watch the creatures because they did such strange things. The shorter ones were putting sand in round containers and moving them all about. Some were building with them. Others were throwing things, walking in the water, and even trying to swim…like an alligator!

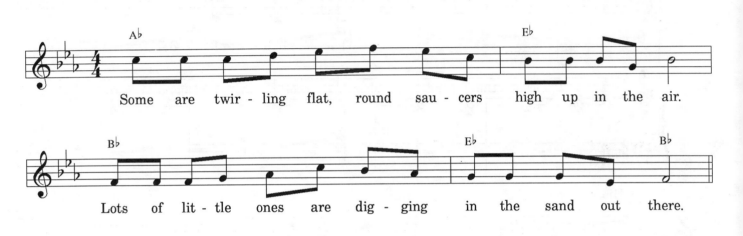

Some are twir - ling flat, round sau - cers high up in the air.

Lots of lit - tle ones are dig - ging in the sand out there.

NARRATOR: He even saw some playing alligator! They were lying in the sand, just like Arlie liked to do.

ARLIE: How very interesting!

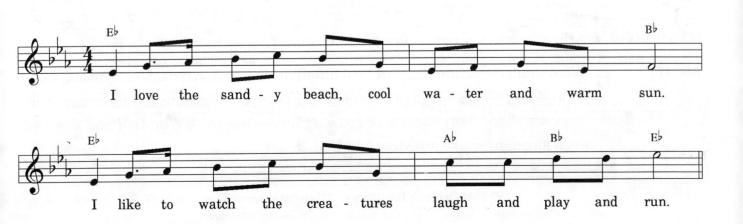

I love the sand - y beach, cool wa - ter and warm sun.

I like to watch the crea - tures laugh and play and run.

What Shall I Do / Daddy Always Taught Me to Bellow

Words and Music by
DEBORAH BEL PFLEGER

What shall I do? I've nev - er been in a sit - u - a - tion like this. What shall I do? I wish I could get a clue. Let me think a mo - ment — or two.

What would my sis-ter do? What would my broth-er do? What would my best friend do? There

must be some way to get my mes - sage a-cross be-fore it's too late!

What would my moth-er do? What would my fath-er do? What would my fath-er do!

Wait! By Gosh! By Gol-ly! I got it! It's true:_____

Dad-dy al-ways taught me to bel-low,———— to bel-low,———— to bel-low!————

Dad-dy al-ways taught me to bel-low!———— "Hey, fel-low,"——— he'd say,

"One day when you grow—— up, my son,———— you will be—— as large as me and you

might find that you'll have the urge——— to say a word——— or two or three."

Dad-dy al-ways taught me to bel-low, ___ to bel-low, ___ to bel-low! ___

Dad-dy al-ways taught me to bel-low! ___ "Hey, fel-low," ___ he'd

say, "Your great, great, great grand - ga-tor ___ was

quite the ___ com-mu-ni - ca-tor. ___ He dis - cov-ered a way to ex-

press what he felt he had to say."

Dad - dy al - ways taught me to bel - low, _____ to bel - low, _____ to

bel - low! _____ Dad - dy al - ways taught me to bel - low, _____ Hey,

fel - low! _____ Bel - low! _____

If It's the Last Thing I Do

Words and Music by
DEBORAH BEL PFLEGER

If it's the last thing I do, I will get through, I would like to com-mu-ni-

cate. Where there's a will there's a way, and I know it's true, I must find out how to re-

late. I un-der-stand, I need a plan, and it might take some time. But I real-ly don't

mind 'cuz there must be much we can share if we on - ly knew

how. If we could on-ly break through the bar-ri-er, I'm sure there's lots in com-mon we could

talk a-bout. And I'll make this a chal-lenge to con-quer,— I'll make this a chal-lenge to

meet. And as long as I be-lieve in my-self and don't give up I'll nev - er see de -

feat. If it's the last thing I do, I will get through, I would

like to com - mu - ni - cate. Where there's a will there's a way, and I

know it's true, I must find out how to re -

late.

Readers' Theater

Production Suggestions

Arlie as **Readers' Theater** is an excellent way to give students public speaking experience. It bridges the gap between *telling a story* and presenting a *full theatrical production*.

Use the **Readers' Theater** script for *Arlie the Alligator* in various ways to enhance students' experiences with the written word. Read it, change it, and expand it to fit your needs.

Prior to reading the script aloud, have students study the parts and discuss what type of voice each character should have.

Isolate the sound effects indicated in the script. Discuss whether it is more effective to read the word or create the sound. Brainstorm ways to create the sound.

Define *verbal expression*. Discuss its importance.

The teacher can read dramatically the entire script, directing the students to respond where "**ALL**" is indicated. This eliminates the pressure for students who are uncomfortable reading aloud and still provides them the opportunity to interact with the written word.

Have students read the entire script in the classroom. Allow students to volunteer for parts. Sometimes the random selection of students for reading parts can be frightening for poorer readers. You may want to encourage those readers to volunteer for parts where more than one person reads at a time, i.e. "**FRIENDS**" or where a sound effect is used. When they become comfortable with the **Readers' Theater** process they may then want to volunteer for individual parts.

Listen to the *Arlie the Alligator* audio tape and one other children's book-on-tape. Compare and contrast the voice techniques used.

List sound effects. List those not used that would contribute to the excitement, understanding, or enjoyment of the tape.

Discuss how music enhances enjoyment of the audio tape. If the music is important to the telling of the story, identify which song performs which job:

gives basic information   identifies a problem or solution
describes a character   shows determination or resolve

Have students practice reading the script aloud, allowing for places where the audience is expected to respond . . . when **ALL** is indicated in the script. Designate one student to present an overview of the story and explain the audience participation parts. Have students write a conclusion communicating friendship and understanding between the groups, classes, etc. Have students brainstorm and create an item . . . warm fuzzy or a balloon, etc. to pass out to the audience at the close of the presentation.

Readers' Theater Script

Readers' Theater Parts

Narrator #1 - 10	Arlie the alligator
Friends	Child
Mother	Father

Narrator 1: Who is the alligator of a different kind?

All: Arlie, Oh Arlie the alligator.

Narrator 2: Who is the one who is so curious to find out everything his mind can hold?

All: Arlie, Oh Arlie, is filled with such curiosity. Oh Arlie, Oh Arlie, where will your adventures lead?

Narrator 3: Who is the alligator always with a smile?

All: Arlie, Oh Arlie the alligator.

Narrator: 4: Who is the one who's there to crawl the extra mile, to share a thought with you and me?

All: Oh Arlie, Oh Arlie, is filled with such curiosity.

Narrator 2: Oh Arlie, Oh Arlie, where will your adventures lead?

Narrator 5: Where will your adventures lead?

Narrator 1: Where will your adventures lead? Arlie!

Narrator 3: Arlie slithered onto the beach to enjoy the warm sun.

Friend: Oh no, Arlie, don't go! You'll get into trouble!

Narrator 4: Arlie paid no attention. *He* loved new experiences and was very curious about the unusual creatures found at the beach. Besides, *he* could take care of *himself.*

Narrator 1: He could hear the laughter of the city folk as they played in the sand nearby.

Narrator 2:   Excitement welled up inside *him* as *he* carefully peered through the tall grass.

Arlie: I love the sandy beach, cool water and warm sun. Hiding behind this reed can be a lot of fun. Watching creatures big and small laugh and play and run. How I wish I could be friends with every single one.

Narrator 3:   Arlie watched for awhile, fascinated by all the different things that *he* saw.

Arlie: What strange creatures they are! All different sizes and shapes.

Narrator 4:   Some are tall, some short, some thin as a reed and some rather portly!

Arlie: Alligators aren't like this at all. They are either short like me, or growing longer like my big brother and sister, or even longer like my Mom and Dad.

Narrator 5:   Arlie knew that *he* would lose *his* beautiful yellow markings when *he* grew up. All alligators do.

Narrator 6:   But otherwise, *he* would look just like all the others.

Narrator 7:   You almost had to be another alligator to tell them apart.

Narrator 8:   *He* loved to watch the creatures because they did such strange things.

Narrator 9:   The shorter ones were putting sand in round containers and moving them all about.

Narrator 10:   Some were building with them.

Narrator 6:   Others were throwing things.

Narrator 7:   . . . walking in the water and even trying to swim . . . like an alligator.

Narrator 8:   Some were twirling flat round saucers high up in the air.

Narrator 9:   Lots of little ones were digging in the sand out there.

Narrator 10:	He even saw some playing alligator! They were lying in the sand, just like **Arlie** liked to do.
Narrator 6:	How very interesting!
Arlie:	I love the sandy beach, cool water, and warm sun. I like to watch the creatures laugh and play and run.
Narrator 7:	SUDDENLY . . . a dark shadow fell across Arlie's path, blocking *his* view.
All:	(Gasping, frightening sounds)
Narrator 8:	Right before *his* eyes were the strangest looking objects *he* had ever seen!
Narrator 9:	Ten round wiggly bumps attached to two towering stalks were staring right into *his* snout!
Arlie:	Oh my! Oh my! What could this be?
Narrator 10:	*He* was too curious to be frightened.
Child:	Hello, Mr. Alligator, what'cha doing?
Narrator 1:	Arlie leaned back as far as *he* could, trying to see where the voice was coming from.
Narrator 2:	*His* heart was pounding loudly.
All:	Thump! Thump! Thump! Thump!
Arlie:	Oh my goodness! It's one of the little creatures!
Child:	I said, hello, Mr. Alligator. What are you doing here?
Arlie:	Oh dear me! I wish I could understand what it is saying. I am sure it is trying to be friends. What should I do? What shall I do?
Narrator 3:	What shall *he* do? *He's* never been in a situation like this.
Narrator 4:	What shall *he* do? I wish I could give him a clue.
Narrator 5:	Let us think a moment or two.
Narrator 6:	What would *his* sister do?

Readers' Theater Reproducible

Narrator 7:	What would *his* brother do?
Narrator 8:	What would *his* best friend do?
Narrator 9:	There must be some way to get *his* message across before it's too late!
Narrator 10:	What would *his* mother do?
Narrator 1:	What would *his* father do?
Arlie:	What would my father do?
All:	Wait! By gosh! By golly! *He's* got it! It's true!
Arlie:	Daddy always taught me to bellow.
All:	To bellow! to bellow!
Arlie:	Daddy always taught me to bellow! "Hey fellow," he'd say!
Father:	One day when you grow up my *son*, You will be as large as me. And, you might find that you'll have the urge . . . To say a word or two or three.
Arlie:	Daddy always taught me to bellow!
All:	To bellow! to bellow!
Arlie:	Daddy always taught me to bellow. "Hey fellow," he'd say.
Father:	Your great, great, great Grand-gator was quite the communicator. He discovered a way to express what he felt he had to say.
Arlie:	Daddy always taught me to bellow!
All:	To bellow! to bellow!
Arlie:	Daddy always taught me to bellow!
All:	Hey fellow. . . . BBEEELLLLOOOOOOOOWWWWWWW!
Narrator 2:	So, Arlie leaned way back,
Narrator 3:	Took a GREAT BIG GIGUNDOUS BREATH,

All:	(inhale loudly)
Narrator 4:	And let out the loudest
All:	BELLLLLOOOOOOWWWWWW
Narrator 4:	. . . anyone had ever heard!
Narrator 5:	It was so loud that all the alligators stopped what they were doing.
Narrator 6:	Even the creatures on the beach turned to look.
All:	**Help! Help! Run for your life! Alligators! Hurry! Let's get out of here!**
Narrator 7:	Arlie's parents moved quickly to *his* side.
Mother & Father:	Arlie, are you all right?
Narrator 8:	At the same time, a larger creature swooped up Arlie's new friend and ran in the opposite direction.
Narrator 9:	Arlie bellowed once more.
Arlie:	Wait! Please wait! Oh, I didn't mean to frighten you!
Narrator 10:	But it was too late. All the creatures were screaming and yelling and running down the beach.
Arlie:	Gosh, I didn't mean to scare anyone.
Mother:	We know that. Other alligators have tried to communicate with the creatures . . .
Father:	But no one has ever gotten through to them. You were very brave to try.
Mother & Father:	We are proud of you.
Mother:	Time for some fresh seaweed pie.
Father:	You've had enough excitement for one day.
Narrator 1:	As *he* paddled off towards home, Arlie looked back one more time.

Division of Creative Learning Consultants © 1993

Narrator 2:	Right then and there, Arlie made a promise to himself . . .
Arlie:	If it's the last thing I do I will get through. I would like to communicate.
Narrator 3:	Where there's a will there's a way, And *he* knows it's true. *He* must find out how to relate.
Arlie:	I understand . . . I need a plan.
Narrator 4:	And it may take some time, but *he* really won't mind.
Narrator 5:	Cuz there must be much *he* can share, if *he* only knew how.
Narrator 6:	If *he* could only break through the barrier, I'm sure there's lots in common *he* could talk about.
Narrator 7:	And *he'll* make this a challenge to conquer.
Narrator 8:	And *he'll* make this a challenge to meet.
Narrator 9:	As long as *he* believes in *himself* and doesn't give up . . .
Narrator 10:	*He'll* never see defeat.
Arlie:	If it's the last thing I do I will get through. I would like to communicate.
AlL:	Where there's a will there's a way, And we know it's true, *he* will find out how to relate!
Arlie:	If it's the last thing I do, I will get through to my friend!
All:	Oh Arlie, Oh Arlie, is filled with such curiosity. Oh Arlie, Oh Arlie, where willl your adventures lead? Where will your adventures lead? Where will your adventures lead?

THE END

A "How-To"

for the
Communication Activities

Communication is "simply" the act of transmitting information. Developing an awareness of the many forms communication can take is more complex. Even so, understanding how human beings communicate is essential. The exercises in the Activities Section include the many ways humans communicate.

Activities are presented in a variety of formats to accommodate learning styles.

✔ Use the *mindMaps* as reference material.

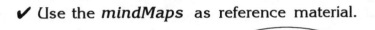

✔ *Class* and *Reference Reproducibles* allow for a common knowledge basis for everyone in the class. Use other *Reproducibles* for individual, partner, or homework.

✔ Use the *Task Cards*

for individually paced activities, Enrichment or in Learning Centers. *The Task Cards can be cut, duplicated, laminated on 5"x8" index cards, and placed in a card file.* Assign one or more activities from each card. Have students consider work from Task Cards for inclusion into Portfolios.

✔ The *Lettered Activities*
A...B...C...D...E...F...G...H...I...J....K...L...M...N...O...P...Q...R...S...T...U...V...

are kernels of ideas for you to expand upon, adding your objectives and tailoring to fit specific needs of your students.

The best educational activities are those that teachers adapt. Reproducibles become teacher-directed discussion questions. Narrative suggestions become cooperative/collaborative learning projects.

Questions become independent study. For this reason, the activities are not age or grade specific.

Spelling and Vocabulary

The words below are in the story *Arlie The Alligator*.

alligator	communicator	swoop	common
situation	attention	reed	container
different	communication	opposite	barrier
bellow	trouble	seaweed	saucer
curiosity	express	fascinated	relate
message	creature	paddle	shadow
adventure	gigundous	portly	conquer
moment	unusual	whisper	stalk
urge	breathe	promise	challenge
slither	peer	strange	snout

1. Choose 9 words. Circle them in **red**. Write them below in alphabetical order. With a partner discuss what your 18 words mean. On the back of this paper use them in a sentence.

1. _____   4. _____   7. _____

2. _____   5. _____   8. _____

3. _____   6. _____   9. _____

2. Choose 3 **other** words. Circle them in **blue**. Below, use each as the *third* word in a sentence. Underline the word in black. Then define the word. For example: unusual—Under the unusual blanket was sand. (different, unique)

1. _____

_____

2. _____

_____

3. _____

_____

Arlie and The "Real" Alligators

Arlie is a *fictitious* alligator. He looks like a real alligator, but he does things that real aligators can't do. Use a dictionary to find the entry word *fictitious*. Read the meaning. In your own words write the meaning of *fictitious*.

_____

Use the word *fictitious* in a sentence.

_____

_____

Draw a picture of a *fictitious* animal.

These characters are *fictitious* in books:

Book Title

Charlotte's Web

Wilbur the pig
Character

Book Title

_____

_____
Character

Book Title

_____

_____
Character

Compare and contrast *Arlie* with "real" alligators.

Similarities	Differences
1._____	1. _____
2._____	2. _____
3._____	3. _____
4._____	4. _____

Alligator Research

When you look up information about something, you are doing *RESEARCH*.

On Your Own or With a Partner—find out what "real" alligators are like. Go to the library and find information about them.

1. Alligators are related to pre-historic animals. Which ones?

_____

2. Alligators live in two countries in the world. What countries are they?

_____

3. How many different kinds of alligators are there? Name them.

_____

_____

_____

4. Why do alligators like to lie in the sun?

_____

_____

5. When alligators are floating on the water they are often mistaken for what kind of objects?

_____

6. When alligators feel frightened, where do they go?

_____

7. *Arlie's* Mom took him home for some fresh seaweed pie. What do "real" alligators eat?

_____

_____

8. What other 3 interesting things did you learn about alligators?

_____

_____

_____

9. In the story, *Arlie* was startled by 10 round wiggly bumps attached to two towering stalks. What were the 10 round wiggly bumps?

_____

10. What kind of feet do alligators have? Draw their footprints.

11. Human beings have two feet. How many feet do alligators have?

_____

12. Human beings have five toes on each foot. How many toes does a human being have?

_____

13. Alligators have a different number of toes on their front feet than on their back feet. How many toes are on their front feet? How many toes are on their back feet?

_____

14. How many toes does an alligator have all together?

_____

15. An alligator's feet help do two important things. Name them.

a. _____

b. _____

16. What helps an alligator swim fast?

_____

17. How fast can an alligator swim?

_____

Answer Key

Compare/Contrast
Possible answers: he has eyelashes, he can think, he can sing, he has feelings, and he tries to talk to the creatures

Research Answer Key
1. Alligators are related to dinosaurs.
2. Alligators live in the United States and China.
3. There are 20 different kinds of alligators.
4. Alligators like to lie in the sun to warm their bodies. They are cold-blooded creatures.
5. When alligators are floating on the water they are often mistaken for an old log.
6. When alligators feel frightened they go into the water.
7. Real alligators eat small flesh animals, insects, crayfish and other small things that live in the water.
8. Answers will vary.
9. The 10 bumps were human toes and the two stalks were human legs.
10. Allligators have webbed feet.
11. Alligators have 4 feet.
12. Humans have 10 toes.
13. Alligators have 5 toes on each front foot. They have 4 toes on each back foot.
14. Alligators have 18 toes.
15. An allligator's feet help them
    a) paddle slowly.
    b) keep their balance in the water.
16. The tail helps an alligator swim fast.
17. An alligator can swim faster than two men can paddle a canoe!

For more information about "real" alligators, consult

Wonders of Alligators and Crocodiles	by W. Blassingame
Biography of an Alligator	by J. Curto
Alligators: An Audubon Reader	by Ada & Frank Graham
Alligators & Other Crocodiles	by R.B. Gross
Who Needs Alligators	by P. Lauber
The American Alligator:	
Its Life in the Wild	by E. Ricciuti
Alligators and Crocodiles	by J. Wexo
Alligators & Crocodiles	by H. Zim

Communication with People

For the Teacher:
Objective: To become aware of different ways humans communicate.

Cooperative Activity:
Divide the class into groups of 4 or 5. Give each group a large sheet of paper. Have a Recorder in each group write *communicate* in a square or circle in the middle of the paper. Then have students, in their own words, define *communicate* or choose a synonym and have the group Recorder write it in the middle. Or distribute the mindMap below.

Next ask each group to mindMap the concept *communicate*. After 5 minutes have groups switch papers and add to the other group's mindMap. Repeat 2 more times. Then return papers to original groups. Have groups discuss new ideas added to their mindMaps.

Enrichment Person to Person: Communicate *without sound.*
Communicate *without hands.*
Communicate *blindfolded.*

FOR THE STUDENT: REFERENCE SAMPLE
✂ ✂ ✂ -

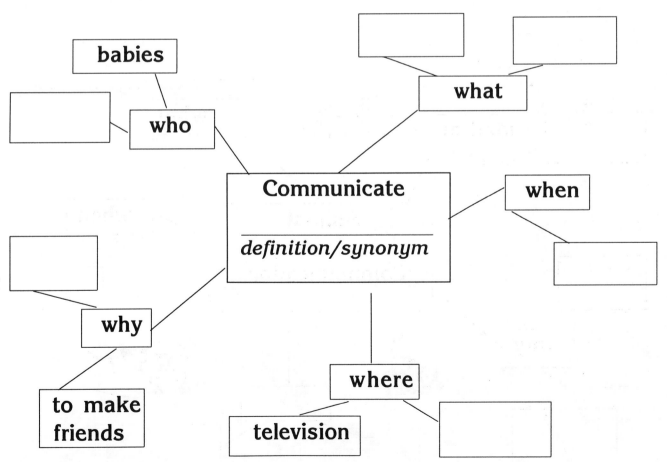

Communication with Animals

Objective: To become aware of different ways animals communicate.

Cooperative Activity:

Divide the class into groups of 4 or 5. Give each group a large sheet of paper. Have a Recorder in each group writie *animal communication* in a square or circle in the middle of the paper. Or distribute the mindMap below.

Next have each group mindMap the concept *animal communication*. After 5 minutes have groups switch papers and add to the other group's mindMap. Repeat 2 more times. Then return papers to original groups. Have groups discuss new ideas added to their mindMaps.

Enrichment:

Compare/contrast the animal communication mindMap with the human communication mindMap. How are they the same? How are they different?

FOR THE STUDENT: REFERENCE SAMPLE:

- -

kind of animal

what

when

Animal Communication

why

Pet Show and Tell

For the Teacher:

Love, friendship, nurturing, caretaking, responsibility, and commnication are virtues children learn through experiences with animals. Integrate lessons relating to animals and pets in a meaningful way.

Objectives: To develop an in-depth knowledge of the pet of their choice.
To communicate knowledge with other students through various projects.
To collaborate and organize a *Pet Show & Tell* to communicate their collective knowledge with others, other classes, or the school and parents.

Activity: A *Pet Show & Tell* can be small or big. It can be done with or without live animals. If you choose not to use live animals make sure students understand that choice from the beginning. If you use animals consider:

Number of pets to be allowed   Type of pets
What will they do in school?   Where will they be kept?
How long will the animals be in school?
What rules need to be made regarding pets in school?

For the Student:

✄ ✄ ✄ -

Pet Show & Tell

Having a *Pet Show & Tell* without
live animals might include:

Posters, Project Displays, and Murals of . . .

wild animals   wild animals that are trainable
domestic animals   pets of students in our class
tricks our pets can do   cost analysis of keeping pets
careers with animals   animals in the movies
animals that help humans   famous animal stories
pets our teachers have   games pets like to play
training techniques used by students in our class

Decide:
Who will you invite to the **Pet Show & Tell**?
Who will write the invitations?   What pets will perform tricks?
Who will be the Master of Ceremonies?   Who will discuss animal training?
Who will make the presentations?   What kind of advertising do you
How many chairs will you need   need?
for guests?

Reproducible

Getting to Know Pets

Task Card 1

1. What kind of pet do you have? If you do not have a pet, what kind of pet would you like to have? _____

2. What is your pet's name? _____

3. On a separate piece of paper draw a picture of your pet.

4. What kind of tricks can your pet do?

_____

✂ -

Task Card 2   *Getting to Know Pets*

1. On a separate piece of paper make a list of all the tricks that the pets of your classmates can do. Divide them into the following categories:
> *Tricks that entertain*
> *Tricks that are helpful*
> *Tricks that are necessary*

2. List techniques to train pets.

_____

3. Prepare a presentation about how you trained your pet—techniques used, how long it took, why did you teach them those things?

✂ - ✂ - - - - - -

Task Card 3   *Getting to Know Pets*

1. Research animals that can be trained and those that cannot be trained.

2. Create a classroom mural of trainable animals. Divide the mural into sections:
   a) Wild animals that cannot be trained   d) Pets of our students
   b) Wild animals that can be trained   e) Tricks our pets can do
   c) Domestic animals

3. Circle the part of the mural you want to work on. On the line write what your job will be for that part of the mural.

For the Teacher — Enrichment Activities for Your Class

A. *Sing animal songs.*

B. *Invite a zoologist to discuss careers that involve working with animals.*

C. *Prepare a presentation: "Things my pet taught me."*

D. *Invite an animal "specialist" to the class as the Special Guest. This could be a veterinarian, jockey, policeman, farmer, park ranger, zookeeper, horse trainer, or someone from the Leader Dog for the Blind and/or Deaf, dog obedience instructor.*

E. *Arrange a visit to a place where animals are trained and/or used to help people.*

   1) Society for blind/deaf

   2) Stables of a police department

   3) Horse farm/riding stable

   4) Dog obedience school

   5) Sea World/amusement park

   6) Zoo—Visit the zoo and talk to the zoologist. What does a zoologist do? What other jobs can you get at a zoo?

   7) National, state or local wildlife park

   8) Circus

Brainstorm questions to ask prior to the visit.

F. *Research animals that make good pets.*

G. *Create a poster, bumper sticker and/or tee-shirt that lists animals that make **GREAT** PETS and animals that DO NOT make good house pets.*

H. *Research and discuss **CAREERS** that involve working with and/or the training of animals.*

I. ***SPECIAL PROJECT** For students interested in a career that involves working with animals, arrange an on-site visit and/or an on-going mentorship relationship with a career person.*

J. *Divide into groups and brainstorm ways that animals HELP humans and other animals.*

K. *Research animals that have been used by the military. What animals are used for national defense?*

L. *Write reports about famous animals in history.*

M. *How do dolphins communicate?*

N. *Review movies that use animals. What laws are there to protect animals that are used in movies?*

O. *Tell about your favorite animal story. What is your favorite animal movie?*

P. *Write an animal story in which the animal is the hero.*

Communicating through Music

Mentorships and shadowing experiences are rewarding for students. So are group presentations. Arrange to have someone visit your school or take your class to musical experiences.

People in music to see:

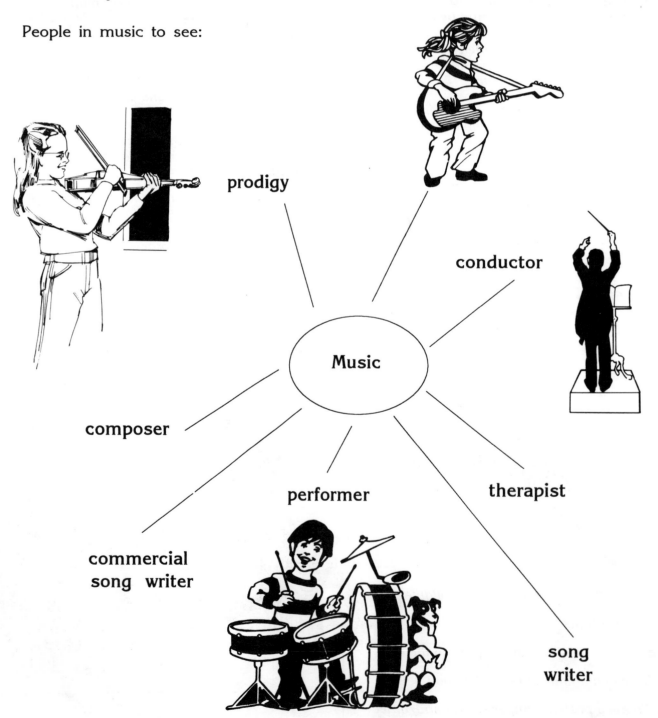

prodigy

conductor

Music

composer

therapist

performer

commercial song writer

song writer

Music & Messages

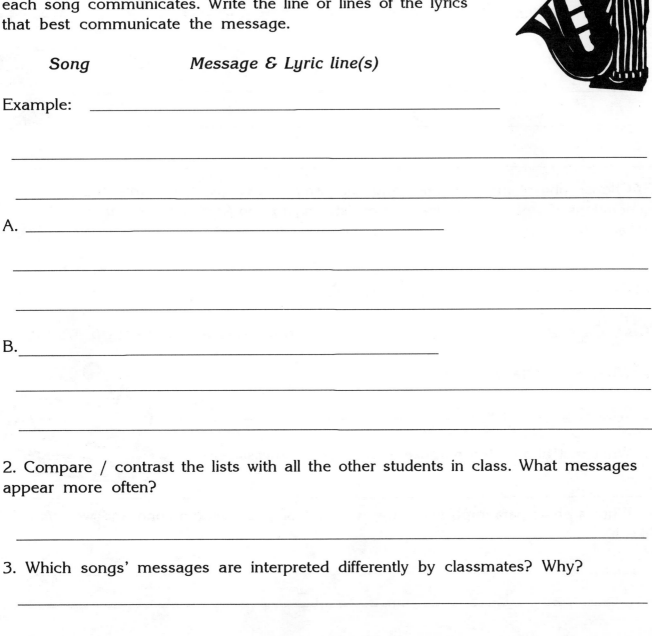

Most songs have a *purpose* or *main idea* or *message*.
Some songs are written just for fun, and some have
an important message. Audiences sometimes find a
purpose different from the song writer's ideas.

1. List two of your favorite songs. Explain the message that
each song communicates. Write the line or lines of the lyrics
that best communicate the message.

        Song   *Message & Lyric line(s)*

Example: _____

_____

_____

A. _____

_____

_____

B. _____

_____

_____

2. Compare / contrast the lists with all the other students in class. What messages
appear more often?

_____

3. Which songs' messages are interpreted differently by classmates? Why?

_____

_____

_____

_____

Task Card 1   *Communicating through Music*

1. Make a list of music titles that communicate the following:
    happiness   fear   patriotism
    love   a message   holidays

2. Use the list. Ask your parents and grandparents to name songs from their youth that fit these categories. Identify the decade and songs.

       Song Title   *Decade*

_____

_____

_____

3. Choose one of the categories and compare/contrast the lyrics from the three generations. What can you learn from listening to song lyrics from different decades?

✂ -

Task Card 2   *Communicating through Music*

1. What is your favorite song? _____

2. Who sings or plays it? _____

3. What is it about? (Its purpose, main idea, or message)

_____

4. Write a short paragraph about the meaning of your favorite song and why you like it.

_____

_____

_____

_____

5. On a separate piece of graph paper use 15 words to create a crossword puzzle of feelings you find in music.

Task Card 3   *Communicating through Music*

Discuss with a partner or in a small group these problems.
Write an essay answer to one of the problems.

1. *Problem* Your grandmother is sick and you want to bring her some music to make her feel better. What type of songs would you bring to her? Name some. Explain your choices.

2. *Problem* Your best friend is having a birthday party and asks you to bring the music. What type of music would you bring and why?

3. *Problem* If you could pick one song that best describes who you are, what would it be? Explain.

4. *Problem* Your party has gotten out of hand. Your parents want you to change the music to calm everyone down. What songs would you use?

5. *Problem* You've been asked to host a party for foreign exchange students. You want to surprise them with music from their homelands. Where might you find out about their native music? Plan music for a party.

✂ -

Task Card 4   *Communicating through Music*

Bring types of music or use music the teacher brings to class. Play one minute of each song. Decide which songs help you respond in the following ways:

Music to study by _____

Music that makes you happy _____

Music that makes you sad _____

Music that makes you want to dance _____

Music to march to in a parade

_____

Music that gives you "goose bumps"

_____

Task Card 5   *Communicating through Music*

1. Plan a visit to a Senior Citizens group (or plan a Great/Grandparents Day) to present a program in song and dance. Research:

    Ages of Senior Citizens   Their favorite songs as children

    Their favorite songs now   The music from their era

    Their favorite songs from school

2. Put together a program of songs and lyrics based on their youth. Include in the program ONE song or poem each that

    is patriotic   is sad

    is romantic   says thanks

    is from a favorite holiday   conveys hope

    they can sing along with   is happy

    is their favorite

✀ -

Task Card 6   *Communicating through Music*

1. With a partner change a nursery rhyme to a Readers' Theater script. Then choose sounds that would make it exciting. Use instruments from the orchestra and anything else to create the sounds.

2. Record an audio tape of the performance. How would you evaluate the effectiveness of the sound effects?

3. Combine the audio tape with pictures and make a video of the story to show younger students.

✀ -

Task Card 7   *Communicating through Music*

1. List the instruments musicians play in an orchestra.

2. Identify which instruments you would use to get the following sounds:

    squeaky   suspenseful

    door opening   rain

    marching   hurrying

    danger

3. List other instruments and the sounds they remind you of.

1. Write poems about the environment. Combine poems with symphonic music to create the mood. Present the music to the class.

2. Write your own music for words to your favorite poem.

3. Write a melody using only one instrument.

4. Listen to an instrumental piece of music several times and write lyrics.

5. Create a "rap" about the environment.

✂ -

Task Card 9   *Communicating through Music*

1. Define *stereotype*.

2. What three **characteristics** do you think of when you think of someone who listens to the following kind of music? Use many descriptive words.

Country-western

Hard Rock

_____   _____

Rock & Roll   Classical

_____   _____

_____   _____

3. What is your favorite kind of music? _____
4. How are you the same as and/or different from the stereotype?
5. If you wanted to tell someone three important things about you, which three songs would you play for them? Why?

Music and Its Lyrics

1. Define *lyrics*. _____

2. Bring sheet music to class or use lyrics of a well-known song. Write the first verse of the lyrics.

_____

_____

_____

3. Compare / contrast lyrics to poetry:

Similarities	Differences

4. Write a verse of lyrics to the melody of *"Row, Row, Row Your Boat."*

_____

_____

_____

_____

5. Write a verse of lyrics with a summer theme to *"Santa Claus is Coming to Town."*

_____

_____

_____

_____

Writing the Music

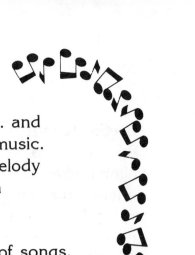

Some song writers hear the music first . . . in their heads . . . and later write the lyrics. Some song writers can only write the music. Some song writers create the words (lyrics) and attach a melody later. Some lyric writers can't write music. Many songs are a *collaboration* between the musician and the lyric writer.

1. Choose a piece of music from a song sheet or in a book of songs.

   Who wrote the lyrics? _____

   Who wrote the music? _____

   What message is the music communicating? _____

2. Choose 3 other songs that are a *collaboration.*

Song Title _____

Music by _____ *Lyrics by* _____

Song Title _____

Music by _____ *Lyrics by* _____

Song Title _____

Music by _____ *Lyrics by* _____

3. Choose 3 other songs that are not a collaboration.

Song Title _____

Music and lyrics by _____

Song Title _____

Music and lyrics by _____

Song Title _____

Music and lyrics by _____ *Class Reproducible*

We Write the Songs . . .

For the teacher:
Objective: To allow students, as a collaborative class activity, to experience the writing of a song by writing lyrics first and then the music. (No music background is required!)

A. *Present an object or subject to the class. Brainstorm attributes. List the attributes on the chalkboard or overhead.*

B. *Specify a theme for the song students are about to write so that the song will have a purpose, message, or theme.*

C. *With the attribute list create the first line, then the second, third and fourth. Point out most song lyrics are often a rhyming poem. As your class argues their way through each line,* they will edit as they go. Indicate that most songs are a collaborative effort and that what they are doing is extremely difficult.

D. *Have the class read the four-line verse aloud several times, experimenting with the rhythm of the words. Use finger snapping and clapping to accent the rhythm. After several attempts, a natural rhythm will emerge.*

E. *With the rhythm established, challenge students to share melodies for the lyrics.*

F. *Allow students to work in groups or with a partner to write music for the lyrics. They can perform it or present an audio tape. (Serious musicians may want more time . . . be flexible.)*

G. *Evaluate and reward participation, not product. Consider extra credit for additional verses.*

H. *Analyze what was written:*
    Did a theme emerge?
    Who would listen to this song? Why?
    How do the lyrics make you feel?
    How does the music make you feel?
    Should anything else be done with this song?

    Extension: Listen to modern-day music. Evaluate it based on the criteria above.

Communicating With Symbols

1. Draw two symbols that are used in school in each category.

Cafeteria Rules

Hallway Rules

Bus Rules

English Rules

2. Create a new symbol for one of the above areas. Explain your reason for creating the symbol.

More Communicating With Symbols

For the teacher:
Objective: To make students aware of the symbols used for daily communication.

Divide the class into small groups. Supply each group with a large piece of paper or the blank mindMap below. Have each group brainstorm and draw in the mind-Map familar symbols for one of the following topics:

Schools   **Sports**   **Careers**   **Feelings**   **Danger**

Have groups rotate their mindMaps to another group after 10 minutes and allow the new group to continue to mindMap the topic. Rotate another time. Then have groups share ideas and questions about the symbols associated with each topic.

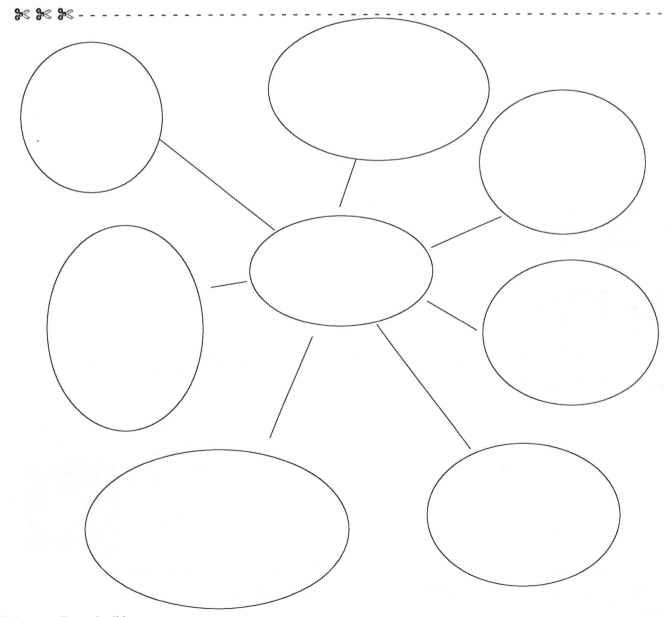

Reference Reproducible

Working With Symbols, Mottos, Flags, and Codes

In a class discussion, small groups, or in partners define, compare and contrast the following words: *symbol, motto, flag, logo, code, trademark, tradition*

✂ -

Task Card 1   SYMBOLS

1. Brainstorm symbols for the following: a) careers b) feelings c) sports

2. List the symbols used in school: a) building related b) subject related—math, English, history, science c) person related.

3. How do symbols help people?

4. Create five symbols to help a person who cannot read complete daily tasks. Identify the task, and draw the symbols.

5. Create a poem, speech, play or song. Present it by using symbols.

6. Play symbol charades. Create symbols and stump the class.

✂ -

Task Card 2   MOTTOS

1. Brainstorm common mottos.

2. Design a class motto and symbol.

3. Display the motto and symbol and explain it to other classes.
✂ -

Task Card 3   FLAGS

1. How many ways can you use flags as symbols?

2. Research your state flag and explain its meaning.

3. Choose two states and research their state flags. How are they like your state flag? How are they different? Design a classroom flag. Explain its meaning.

Reproducible

Task Card 4

1. How do different cultures use different symbols to show
a) family   b) marriage   c) age   d) occupation

2. How do we use clothing as symbols?

3. How are objects and animals used as symbols to represent a country?

4. What part does tradition play in the symbols that we wear?

- -

Task Card 5

1. What is Morse Code?

2. Why is it important to have secret codes?

3. Research secret codes. Develop your own code. Exchange a coded message and decode it. In poster form explain your secret code to the class.

4. In what circumstances are secret codes used today?

5. Explain ways to use secret codes for protection.

6. What does this Morse Code spell?

Communicating through Spoken Language

The most common form of communication people use is verbal sounds. Verbal sounds can take on a variety of forms from differences in languages to tonal changes (high and low), levels of expression and volume, singing, or just making noises. Verbal communication is as different as the number of people on the planet.

FOR THE STUDENT:

✂ -

Define *verbal.* MindMap ways people use verbal sounds to communicate.

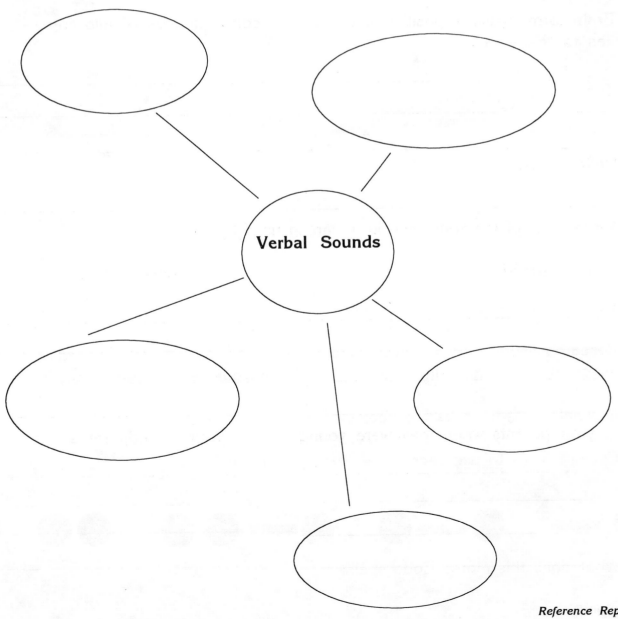

Growing Up with Language

1. Make a list of all of the "baby words" spoken in your family or in your neighbors' homes.

_____ _____
_____ _____
_____ _____
_____ _____
_____ _____

Create a *"Baby's First Words"* Dictionary.

2. Brainstorm possible positive and negative consequences of allowing babies to "baby talk."

_____
_____
_____

3. Define *slang*.

_____

4. Make a list of the slang and its meaning used by:

your friends

_____
_____
_____
_____

your parents today

_____
_____
_____
_____

your parents when they were young

_____
_____
_____

your grandparents

_____
_____
_____

5. Make a dictionary of 10 *"Kid-Terms"* to help adults understand what you—the younger generation—is saying.

Term   *Meaning*

1. _____

2. _____

3. _____

4. _____

5. _____

6. _____

7. _____

8. _____

9. _____

10. _____

6. See how many words you can list whose *dictionary* meaning is different or opposite from its *usage* meaning. For example, *"BAD"*.

_____

_____

_____

_____

7. Use your collection of "slang" terms in a poem or story.

Class Reproducible

For the Teacher . . . the Spoken Word

Foreign Language

A. *Determine the number of bilingual children in your classroom or school. How many different languages are spoken in your home? Your classroom? At school?*

B. *Invite persons speaking foreign languages into the classroom. Ask students to share various ethnic greetings they use in their homes. See how many ways you can learn to say:*
Hello!   How are you?
Thank you for coming.   Good-bye!

Tone of Voice

A. *How can the "tone" of your voice create different meanings? Give examples.*

B. *Using different tones, say "Hello. How are you?" to convey the following feelings:*
love, friendship, hate, anger, impatience, anxiety, excitement, frustration and shyness

Careers

A. *Research various occupations and make a list of the "language" used on the job. Include spoken as well as signals used. For example: computer language: disks, monitors, boot*
Author: galley proof, manuscript, quote

B. *Invite to class an actor trained in "voice-over" work for television and radio. Have them discuss the techniques they need for this occupation. Discuss the differences between "hard sell" and "soft sell." Create a one minute commercial and tape it using a "hard sell" approach and a "soft-sell" voice.*

C. *Explore occupations/careers that exist in the language field. See how many you can list.*

Dialect

A. *Define dialect. What dialects are common in your area? What does a dialect tell about a person? List advantages and disadvantages of speaking with a dialect.*

Public Speaking

A. *What is "public speaking?" It is known to be feared by most people. For what reasons do you think this is?*

B. *List negative and positive feelings about being asked to stand up and give a speech. Next to each negative feeling write a technique for overcoming that feeling.*

C. *List occupations that require public speaking skills.*

D. *List the characteristics of a good public speech.*

E. *Write a one-minute speech about yourself.*

Research

A. *Study the principles of debate. Divide into groups. Debate the pros and cons of one of the fairy tales.*

    Little Red Ridinghood: *Burglar* or *Victim?*

    The Big Bad Wolf: *Murderer* or *Misunderstood Neighbor?*

    Hansel & Gretel: *Thieves* or *Kidnap Victims?*

B. *What do you say when you don't know what to say? Talking to strangers is not easy for most people. Share opening questions that you can use with anyone to start a conversation.*

The Art of Communication

A. *Brainstorm appropriate responses to the following*

    a distant relative sends you a gift
    the neighbor saves your cat who was stuck in a tree
    your best friend stays home from a special event to help you study
    you see someone drop their wallet
    you want to borrow your best friend's favorite sweater

The Art of Conversation

A. *Practice different ways to introduce someone:*

    yourself to a new neighbor
    yourself to a group you just joined
    your parents to your new friend
    your best friend to your grand-parents

Communicating through Visual & Performing Arts

Visual and performing arts are the "life form" of communication. From the beginning of time man used signs and symbols to send a message, tell a tale, converse or worship. Visual and performing arts reflect day to day life or life as the artist perceives it should be. When we study history we always look to the art from that era for clues about everyday life.

Have students define *art, visual arts, commercial arts.*

VISUAL ARTS

A. *List ways we communicate through the visual arts.*

B. *Brainstorm careers in the visual arts. What education is necessary to go into those careers? What hobbies will help?*

C. *Visual arts affect the way we feel. Find 10 magazine or newspaper photographs that show different feelings.*

D. *How can visual arts help people to feel better about themselves?*

E. *What visual arts are used in your school? In your classroom?*

F. *What visual arts are hanging in your bedroom that reflect your interests?*

G. *Create something visual that is humorous. Design a visual arts project that will make someone laugh.*

H. *What can you learn about someone by the art that they like?*

I. *Visit local artists and watch them work. Find out as much as possible about them: philosophy, background, experience, when they first became interested in art, what their childhood was like, their favorite media, and their aspirations.*

J. *List as many kinds of artists as you can. Pick one and write a report. For example: oil painter, water color artist, portrait artist, portrait photographer, sculptor, metal expert, weaver.*

K. *List kinds of art you have in your home.*

L. *List kinds of art in your classroom.*

M. *Explain why color, texture and line are important in art.*

N. *Create a vocabulary list of art terms.*

O. *Visit illustrators and discuss how and where their ideas come from.*

COMMERCIAL ART

A. *Visit a commercial art studio. Learn what they do. Invite a commercial artist into your classroom.*

B. *Create a poster that sells something—an idea, a concern or a product.*

ART

A. *What are the primary colors?*

B. *What messages do colors communicate?*

C. *List warm and cool colors.*

D. *List ways teachers can use art in school to motivate kids.*

E. *What can we tell about a person by the colors that they wear?*

F. *If you want to have a room where you want people to come and relax, what color/s would you paint it?*

G. *What color would you paint a room that is used for lots of activities? Explain your choice.*

H. *How are colors used to identify things?*

I. *What are your school colors? Why have school colors?*

J. *How are our interests in art influenced by television, radio, and other forms of technology?*

K. *What technology influences your taste in art?*

L. *Design a poster that answers the statement: **Art is** . . .*

M. *Discuss ways illustrations in children's books can influence young children in negative ways; in positive ways.*

N. *In what ways can art help people who have poor self-esteem?*

O. *Illustrate books written by first graders. Pair older students with younger students.*

P. *How do psychologists use art to evaluate patients?*

Q. *How do lawyers and policeman use art?*

R. *What is propaganda? How can art be used in propaganda?*

S. *What is subliminal art? Give examples. Why are some people upset about using it?*

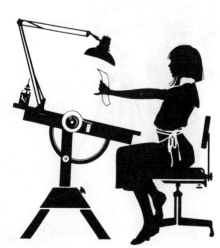

PHOTOGRAPHY

A. *Photography is a form of art. Brainstorm ways we use photography to communicate.*

B. *How many kinds of photographers are there? List them. How are their jobs smiliar? How are they different?*

C. *Brainstorm careers in photography. What education is necessary to become a photographer?*

D. *Invite three different kinds of photographers to speak to your class. Prepare questions related to their type of work. For example, invite a newspaper photographer, commercial photographer, company photographer, portrait photographer, police/crime photographer.*

DANCE

A. *Dance is a performing art. How many different kinds of dance can you think of?*

B. *Brainstorm careers in dance. What education is necessary to become a dancer?*

C. *Create an illustrated vocabulary list of dance terms.*

D. *How does dance help people?*

E. *Research the names of the dances your grandparents do or did; your parents.*

F. *What are the dances of today called? What are your favorite dances?*

G. *What is interpretive dance? Choreograph your own dance.*

H. *Show by demonstraton a dance that can be used to help someone.*

I. *Study your own nationality and present a report, video or pictures of costumes and dances representing your ethnic origins.*

J. *Discuss traditional dances used at special occasions.*

K. *Choreograph a dance that conveys a strong emotion.*

L. *Choreograph a dance that projects a message.*

THEATER

A. Create a puppet that represents how you feel in school.

B. Write, create the puppets and perform a play that presents a problem and a solution.

C. Sight examples of favorite puppets on television.

D. Invite a puppeteer into you classroom to speak about creating, making and performing in this field.

E. How are puppets used to help people?

F. How do police departments use puppets?

G. How do psychologists use puppets?

H. What can we learn about people from puppets?

I. Write a play about school that tells younger students what to expect.

J. Actors and actresses communicate feelings by taking on the role of someone else. Perform a nursery rhyme.

K. Visit a local acting school, theater or college theater department. Discuss acting techniques that project an image.

L. Discuss techniques actors use to remember their lines. Try them using a poem or script from a play.

M. Go to a play. Then go backstage after the performance to see how a production is put together.

N. Produce "Arlie The Alligator" or another children's play for the primary grades in your school.

O. List questions you would ask a playwrighter. Then interview a playwriter about writing for the theater.

P. List questions you would ask a scriptwriter. Then interview a scriptwriter about writing for television and films.

Q. Write a one minute script for a commercial communicating a concern and a solution. Stage, produce and video tape it.

PANTOMIME

A. What is pantomime? Where did it originate?

B. Watch a movie or video about pantomime. Why do you think people are so fascinated by pantomime?

C. Create a pantomime about your favorite book character. Have the rest of the class guess who you are and what you are trying to say.

D. To play charades you use a form of pantomime. Write directions to play charades. Then brainstorm topics. Play charades using the topics.

Communicating through Body Language

Task Card 1

1. Define *body language.* On another piece of paper draw a picture without words that defines *body language.*
2. In a group of 3 brainstorm ways these parts of our bodies can send messages:

Hands

Eyes

Arms

Lips

✂ -

Task Card 2   *Body Language*

1. *Charades!* Divide into groups of 3. List 5 feelings our bodies can, without talking, communicate to others and how our body might communicate those feelings. Put each group's ideas into a hat. Then, individually, draw one idea out of the hat and act it out. Have class members guess the feeling.

2. Using only your hands and arms, communicate the following:

HELLO	GOOD-BYE	COME HERE	GO AWAY
OKAY	GREAT JOB	PEACE	CALL YOUR DOG
CHOKING	HAPPINESS	EXCITEMENT	THANK YOU
OH NO!	SHOW ANGER		

3. On a separate piece of paper define the following. What positive and negative emotion does each suggest?

good posture	swagger	bad posture	walk
skip	run	shuffle	slouch

1. Brainstorm five things you can learn about people by the way they walk.

2. Create and demonstrate a walk for the following:

Happy   Sad   Excited   Old
Frightened   Tired   a Cowboy   an Athlete
Someone who is poor   Someone who is rich
Someone who is shy   Someone who is stuck-up

3 Using only your face, demonstrate the following:

Anger   Hate   Love   Embarrassment
Happiness   Sickness   Sadness   Nervousness

4. Discuss if it is easy to tell how someone feels by the way they look. Why or why not? Give an example of a time when it is *easy* to tell how someone feels. Give an example of a time when it is *hard* to tell how someone feels.

5. What are some ways to determine how someone *really* feels?

✂ -

1. Cut from newspapers and magazines pictures of people expressing all kinds of emotions, positions and occupations. Exchange your pictures with someone else from your class. Write a short paragraph about three of the pictures.

    Explain:
    a. what emotions you see and feel when you look at the picture.
    b. what things about the picture give you clues to the feelings expressed.
    c. what you think the situation is.

2. Then write a story about what happened *after* the picture was taken.

3. People can tell how you feel by the way you sit. Sit in your chair as if you felt:

a) anger   b) nervous   c) sick   d) happy
e) tired   f) shy   g) beautiful   h) ugly

What You See Isn't Always What Is!

A. *Find a newspaper or magazine story that has an accompanying photograph.*

B. *Before reading the story—
In groups have students:*

*— describe the person physically and emotionally
— decide if the person has a family
— if there are other persons in the photo decide if they are all related and if so, how
— if the relationship among the people influences what is happening in the picture
— describe what is happening and what led up to the action they see
— suggest a solution or consequence to the action in the picture.*

C. *On the chalkboard or overhead divide the space into four columns. Label them*

**emotions   relationships
action   solutions/consequences**

D. *Have a member of each group write what the group has determined about the picture in the appropriate column.*

E. *After recording the classes' views, read the story that accompanied the picture. Discuss how accurately the groups interpreted the photograph. Discuss what body language clues led them to believe what they did. Discuss the accuracy of believing what you see.*

F. *Have the groups or individuals write a poem or a story about what they see.*

Beaver Valley News—Monday Dec.1

Missing Girl is Found!

Communicating through "Sign" Language

For the Teacher:

Signs are a part of our everyday existence.
A. Have students list as many signs as possible that help them in school.
B. Then have groups of students brainstorm ways signs are used to help people.
C. Brainstorm signs used to protect animals.
D. Have students create a "sign" without using names that tells who they are.

✂ -

Task Card 1   *Native American Sign Language*

1. In the library find out about Indian Sign language used by native American Indians. How many different kinds of Indian sign languages are there?

2. Native American Indians use several means to express themselves. List three and give an example of each.

3. Work in small groups or with partners to create a greeting or message you can relay in a particular Native American sign language.

4. Create an alphabet book or a game for young children using a Native American sign language.

✂ -

Task Card 2   *"Global Signing"*

1. Research sign language our military personal use. How many different signs and symbols are used by the military?

2. What signs are used to communicate with other military personnel?

3. What signs are used to communicate with foreign countries?

Reproducible

Task Card 3 — *Communication for the Physically Challenged*

1. Using library books and information from national organizations, research ways physically challenged people communicate.

2. Develop a "new" system of communicating basic needs for someone:

    a) who suddenly loses their hearing
    b) who loses the ability to talk

3. To simulate hard of hearing, the teacher will "block" the hearing of 1/2 the class for one hour. The other half will read a story speaking in whispers. The hard of hearing students will record how they felt and what they learned.

    The teacher will repeat the experience with the other 1/2 of the class.

    Discuss feelings and frustrations of being physically challenged.

✂ - ✂ -

Task Card 4 — *Communication for the Hard of Hearing*

1. Learn sign language for the deaf.

2. Invite a deaf person to come to your classroom and talk to you. Prepare questions using sign language.

3. To simulate how it feels not to hear, watch a movie/video in the classroom without the sound. Write the story. See how many words you think you understood by reading lips. Discuss how important expressions and body language became to the communication process.

4. Tell a joke in sign language.

5. What other senses would you have to rely on more strongly if you no longer could hear?

1. Labels are signs that tell us something about a person, place or thing. Look around the room and see how many labels you can see. List them.

2. List all the reasons to label things and all the reasons *not* to label things. Then with a partner debate the *necessity* for labeling things.

3. Design a better label for a product that you want your mom to buy.

4. Write a *funny* story about what happens when someone puts the wrong label on a product.

5. Create a cartoon about misunderstanding the meaning of a label.

6. Sometimes we put labels on people. List labels that people like. List labels that people don't like.

✂ -

Task Card 6   *Communication In Careers*

1. Choose three occupations that use a kind of sign language. Explain what they use. (Example: Orchestra conductors use batons.)

2. Think of jobs where hand signals are used to communicate.

3. The following jobs use what objects to communicate: ship's captain, school crossing guard, police officer, quarterback on the football team, train conductor.

4. Create a hand signal . . .
    a) to ask for quiet
    b) to announce recess time
    c) to put your books away
    d) to announce time to line up
    e) to ask students to sit down

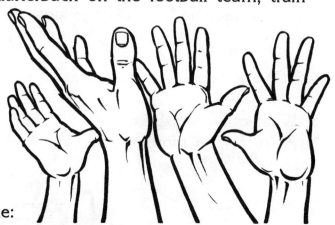

5. Show hand signals in a baseball game: by the players, by the umpire, by the coach, by the crowd.

Reproducible

Communicating through Writing

The written word is a powerful form of communication. Committing thoughts, ideas and words to the printed page makes them come alive.

When teaching children to communicate through the written word, remember that writing is a two-part process—grammar makes up one important aspect, and creative ideas, thoughts and feelings complete the process. Plan your curriculum to develop *both* skills. Good resources to build grammar skills and the creative process are *It's About Writing* (Pieces of Learning—Creative Learning Consultants Inc.,) and *You Are the Editor.* (Fearon)

Children of all ages can write if they can think. Older students can write down young children's ideas on memo cube sheets and then the younger children can physically manipulate their ideas in their mindmaps to develop their products.

IDEAS TO MAKE WRITING FUN —
a) Give students a choice of products: story, poem, song, etc.
b) Make writing assignments relevant! Involve students in the process.
c) Write with Music! Use it as background or make it an integral part of the assignment.

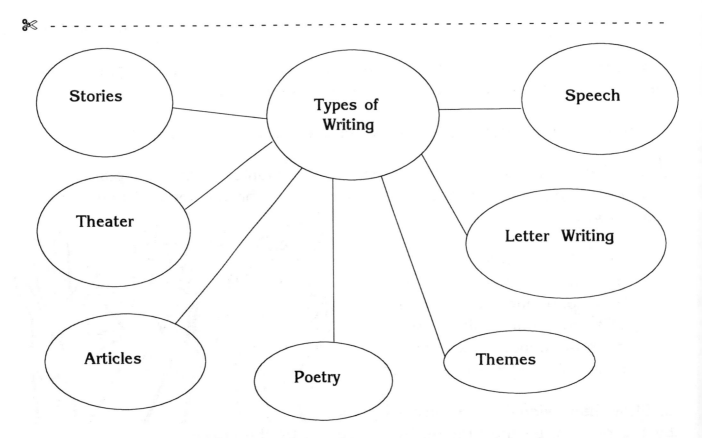

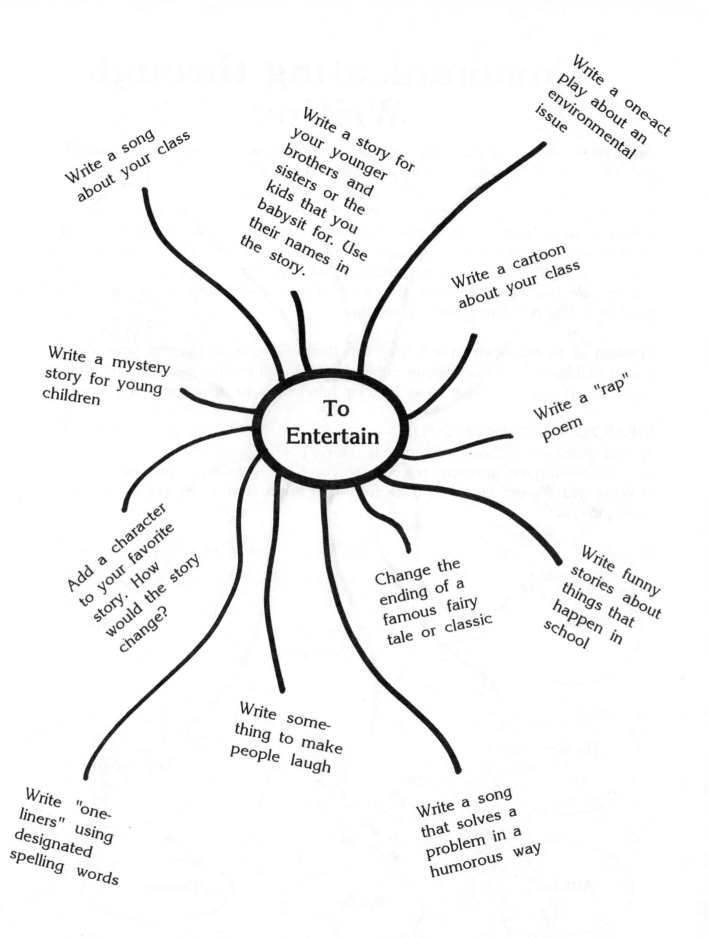

Write a one-act play about an environmental issue

Write a story for your younger brothers and sisters or the kids that you babysit for. Use their names in the story.

Write a song about your class

Write a cartoon about your class

Write a mystery story for young children

To Entertain

Write a "rap" poem

Add a character to your favorite story. How would the story change?

Change the ending of a famous fairy tale or classic

Write funny stories about things that happen in school

Write something to make people laugh

Write "one-liners" using designated spelling words

Write a song that solves a problem in a humorous way

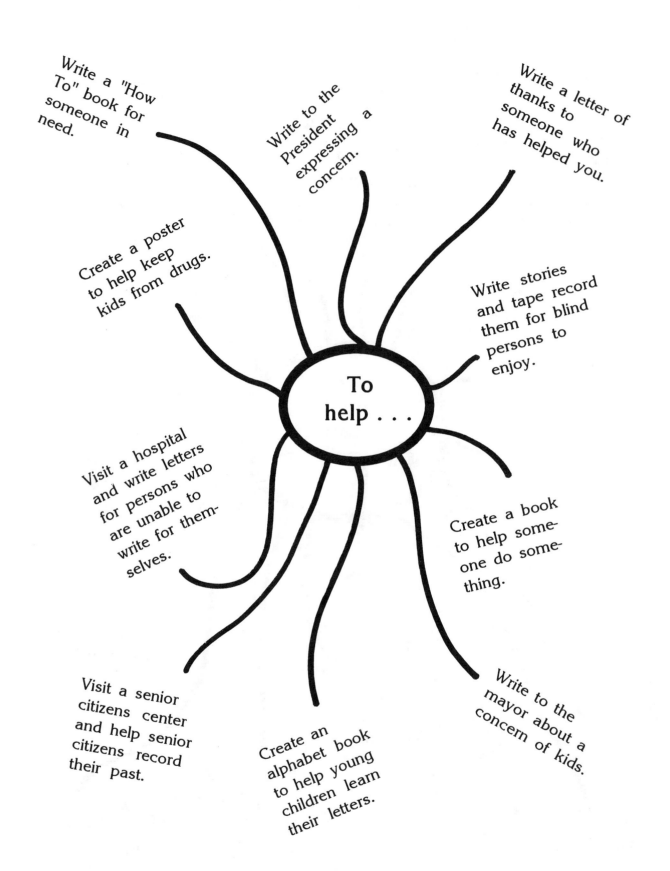

Write a "How To" book for someone in need.

Write to the President expressing a concern.

Write a letter of thanks to someone who has helped you.

Create a poster to help keep kids from drugs.

Write stories and tape record them for blind persons to enjoy.

To help . . .

Visit a hospital and write letters for persons who are unable to write for themselves.

Create a book to help someone do something.

Visit a senior citizens center and help senior citizens record their past.

Create an alphabet book to help young children learn their letters.

Write to the mayor about a concern of kids.

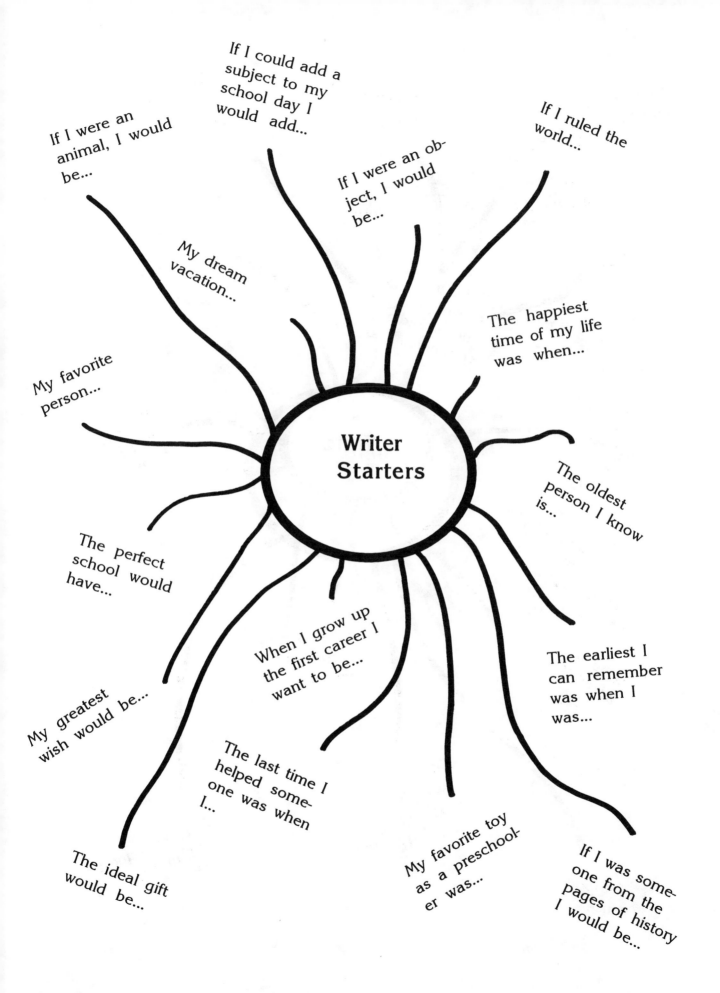

If I could add a subject to my school day I would add...

If I were an animal, I would be...

If I were an object, I would be...

If I ruled the world...

My dream vacation...

The happiest time of my life was when...

My favorite person...

Writer Starters

The oldest person I know is...

The perfect school would have...

When I grow up the first career I want to be...

The earliest I can remember was when I was...

My greatest wish would be...

The last time I helped someone was when I...

My favorite toy as a preschooler was...

The ideal gift would be...

If I was someone from the pages of history I would be...

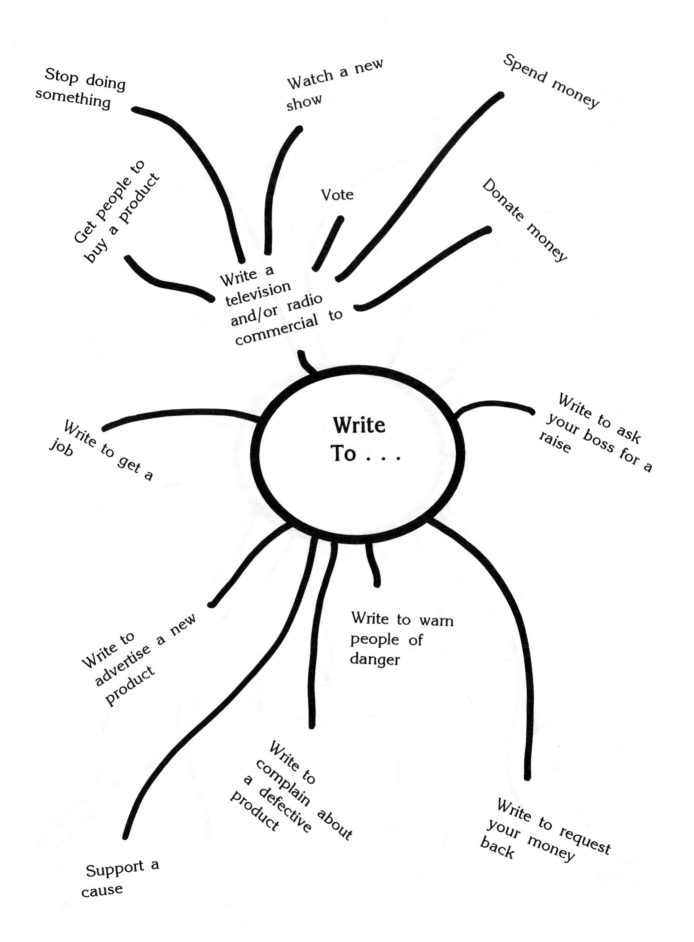

Stop doing something

Watch a new show

Spend money

Get people to buy a product

Vote

Donate money

Write a television and/or radio commercial to

Write To . . .

Write to get a job

Write to ask your boss for a raise

Write to advertise a new product

Write to warn people of danger

Write to complain about a defective product

Write to request your money back

Support a cause

To explain a problem

To recommend someone for an award

To a "special" friend thanking them for a nice evening

To a relative

To order something

To a friend

That express sympathy for a death in the family

That apologize for something

Write Letters . . .

To a politician, organization, corporation, to express a concern

To ask for information

To end a relationship

To tell someone to stop "bugging" you

To get a job

To cancel an engagement

That express a feeling

To become a member of a group

That thank someone for a kindness

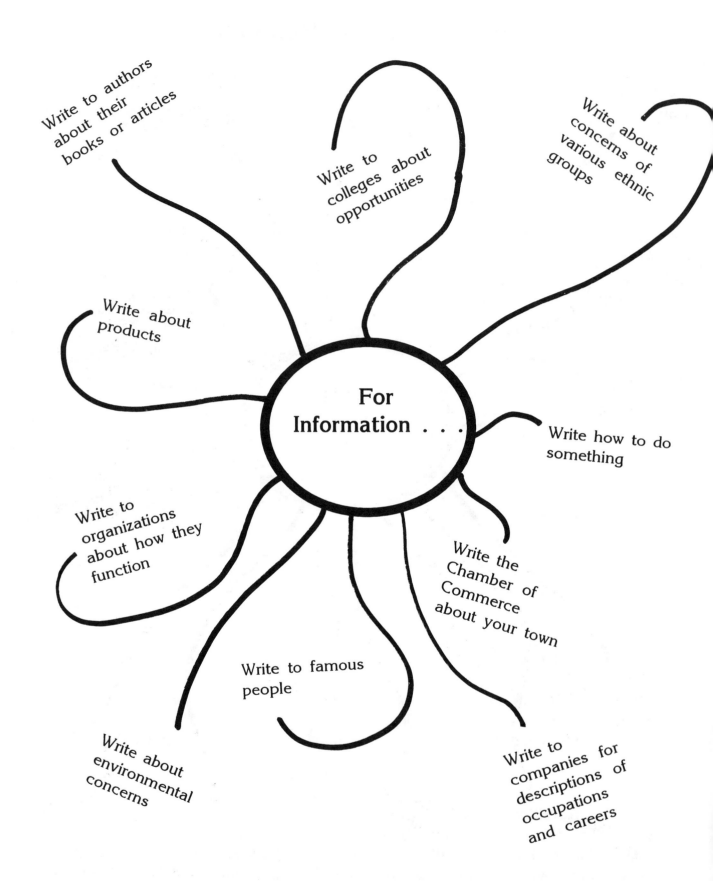

Write to authors about their books or articles

Write to colleges about opportunities

Write about concerns of various ethnic groups

Write about products

For Information . . .

Write how to do something

Write to organizations about how they function

Write the Chamber of Commerce about your town

Write to famous people

Write about environmental concerns

Write to companies for descriptions of occupations and careers

Bibliography & Resources

Arlie the Alligator

Arlie the Alligator *by Sandra Warren* — a beautiful four-color hardback story book complete with Arlie's open-ended story, illustrations, lyrics and sheet music.   *$13.95*

Arlie's story on the audio cassette **Arlie the Alligator** *with music by Deborah Bel Pfleger*. For listening, reading, and singing along with Arlie and his friends.
                                        $5.95

Order from

Arlie Enterprises
PO Box 360933, Strongsville OH 44136.
$3 S/H or 10% above $30
Ohio residents add 7% sales tax

Arlie **the Alligator**

Written by Sandra Warren
Music by Deborah Bel Pfleger   Illustrated by Deborah Thomas

Arlie Enterprises

Indian Sign Language

Amon, A., **Indian Sign Language**, Doubleday & Co., Inc., 1968.
Fronval, G., and Dubois, D., **Indian Signs & Signals**, Oak Tree Press Co., 1978.
Tomkins, W., **Indian Sign Language**, Dover Publications Inc., 1969.

Hearing Impaired

Aseltine, L., Mueller, E., and Tait, N., **I'm Deaf and It's Okay**, Albert Whitman & Co., 1986.
Chaplin, S., **I Can Sing My ABC's**, Kendall Green Publications, 1986.
Greene, L., and Dicker, E., **Interpreting Sign Language**, Franklin Watts, 1989.
Lane, L., **The Gallaudet Survival Guide to Signing**, Gallaudet University Press, 1987.

Theatrical / Musical

Bauer, C.F., **Presenting Readers' Theater**, H.W. Wilson Co., 1987.
Berger, M., **The Science of Music**, Thomas Y. Cravell, 1989.
Howard, V., **Pantomimes, Charades & Skits**, Sterling Publishing Co., Inc., 1969.
Palmer, G., and Loyd, N. **Music Tells the Tale**, Frederick Warne & Co., 1967. Roets, Lois, **Readers Theater Volumes** *I—General Interest* *II—Famous People* *II—Entrepreneurs* Leadership Publishers, Des Moines IA 1992.

Pieces of Learning

Don't Burn Down the Birthday Cake Poems that celebrate childhood experiences while gently focusing on human values. Words and pictures stimulate the imagination, enhance self-concept, and encourage self-awareness. *by Joe Wayman*
CLC0006   All ages   96p. Hardback   ISBN 0-945799-00-4   **$13.95**

If You Promise Not to Tell helps kids find that poetry is a friend. This collection invites you back to childhood and opens a door to the friends, the fears, and the joys of growing up. *by Joe Wayman*
CLC0040   All ages   96p. Hardback   ISBN 0-945799-04-7   **$13.95**

The Birthday Cake and **If You Promise Not To Tell Discussion Guides** use the poems as a springboard for discussion. Help children explore their feelings as well as experience a more positive sense of self. *by Joe Wayman*
CLC0007   **Cakes**   ISBN 0-945799-01-2   **$5.95**
CLC0099   **Promise**   ISBN 0-945799-05-5   **$5.95**

The Birthday Cake AUDIO CASSETTE of the poems read aloud by *Joe Wayman* and *Nancy Johnson* will delight your class or family.
CLC0008   All ages   All poems from the book   **$12.95**

I Like Me ACTIVITY BOOK offers lyrics and music as well as reproducible activities for 15 children's songs. Activities encourage creativity, enhance self-esteem, provide for cooperative work, and promote language skills and critical thinking. Reproducibles. *by Joe Wayman*
CLC0036   K-8   36 p.   ISBN 0-945799-02-0   **$7.95**
CLC0037   **AUDIO CASSETTE**   K-8   15 songs   **$9.95**

Colors of My Rainbow ACTIVITY BOOK Lyrics and activities for 10 color songs and the feelings each color brings to mind. Great resource for writing and the fine arts teacher. Reproducibles. *by Joe Wayman*
CLC0012   K-8   36p.   ISBN 0-945799-03-9   **$7.95**
CLC0013   **AUDIO CASSETTE**   K-8   10 songs   **$9.95**

Pieces of Learning

The Faces of Gifted explores identifying, understanding, and responding to the gifted child. Topics include right/left hemisphere functions, creativity, discipline, communication, gifted children at risk, preschool gifted children, gifted girls, school setting, and parent advocacy. Reproducibles. Complements the video **Parenting Skills for the 90s:** *Your Gifted Child. by Nancy Johnson*
CLC0086   K-12   112 p.   ISBN 0-9623835-0-3   **$9.95**

Parenting Skills for the 90s: Your Gifted Child (VHS) is a 3 segment, 90-minute video addressing characteristics of gifted children, techniques for surviving the joys and frustrations of having a gifted child, and communication skills critical to positive interaction with this decade's gifted learners. Complements the book **The Faces of Gifted**. *by Nancy Johnson*
CLC0098   90 min VHS   ISBN 0-9623835-1-1   **$29.95**

Positive Power For Families This "Read together" story explores family reactions and responses to behaviors through humor and a storyline. The authors present a "workable system for achieving love and harmony in a family." The book offers parents insights and practical strategies as it "looks at discipline in a positive way." *by Anne & Gary Wakenhut*
CLC0142   All families   64p.   ISBN 1-880505-03-7   **$8.95**

Parenting Skills for the 90s: The Parenting Puzzle: Piece by Piece (VHS) is a 90 minute, 2 segment interactive seminar. The first segment focuses on the parent as role model and teacher. The second segment explores life long learning. Focus on traditions, consistency, secrets, problems, heroes, responsibility, overparenting, safe rebellion, health and other 90s' attitudes and concerns. Useful for In-home viewing & Parent In-service. *by Nancy Johnson*
CLC0116   All families   90 min VHS   ISBN 1-880505-00-2   **$39.95**